G000274153

1 A hobbyhorse of *c.* 1820 with a suitably-clad rider. This photograph was taken at a Malvern Carnival celebrating Queen Victoria's Diamond Jubilee and the dashing young buck astride the machine is Walter Santler, one of two brothers who founded a cycle-manufacturing business in Malvern Link in 1885 and were later pioneers in the motor industry

2 *Frontispiece, overleaf* All the dignity of the Captain of a respected tricycle club is revealed in this picture. J. F. Santonna, of the Worcester Tricycle Club, poses with his machine, *c.* 1886. Note the formal quasi-military style of the C.T.C.-recommended uniform

Victorian and Edwardian

CYCLING & MOTORING

from old photographs

Introduction and commentaries by

A. B. DEMAUS

B. T. Batsford Ltd · *London*

Reprinted 1983
First published 1977

ISBN 0 7134 0556 2

Phototypeset by Tradespools Ltd, Frome, Somerset
Printed by The Anchor Press Ltd,
and bound by William Brendon & Son Ltd,
both of Tiptree, Essex
for the publishers B T Batsford Limited
4 Fitzhardinge Street, London W1H 0AH

Contents

Acknowledgment

The author is greatly indebted to his many friends who have aided and abetted his love of early motoring and cycling over the course of many years and, in particular, to those individuals and institutions who have provided him with the photographs from which this selection has been made. The sources of the photographs selected are listed below.

Although very many people have generously given of their knowledge of early cycling and motoring in helping the author to prepare this book, he must particularly thank D. C. Field, DFH, C.Eng., MIEE, Research Historian of The Veteran Car Club of Great Britain, and G. N. Georgano, Photographic Librarian of the National Motor Museum, Beaulieu, for their invaluable help in identification and dating of 'problem' pictures.

1, 18, 41, 87 F. W. Ring-Santler; 2, 27 C. A. Hawkes; 3 A. J. Santonna; 4, 30, 31 The Editor, *The Boneshaker*; 5 Kidderminster Public Library; 6 Royal Worcester Porcelain Works, Ltd.; 7, 17, 39, 56, 62, 65, 67, 72, 73, 80–2, 86, 88, 131, 140–2, 153–5 Hereford Record Office; 9, 152 Ludlow Museum; 14, 23, 24, 33, 45, 76, 91, 92, 104, 113–16, 118, 120–2, 126, 134, 135 Worcester Record Office; 11, 46, 54, 84, 93 B. Butcher; 12, 13, 15, 25 W. A. Bush; 16, 28, 32, 58 R. Townsend; 19, 37 Malvern Public Library; 20, 34, 35, 50, 52, 53, 69, 89, 90, 97, 102, 107, 108, 110, 113, 119, 123, 124, 125, 127, 138, 139, 145, 146, 148–50 The Publishers; 22 Elgar Birthplace Museum; 10, 21 D. Irvine; 26 Worcester St. John's C.C.; 29, 42, 43, 47, 64, 106, 159 The Hon. J. A. H. Wallace; 36, 48, 49, 59, 63, 68, 70, 144 L. F. Barham; 38 J. A. Clark; 40 Mrs. G. Ahern; 44, 57 Miles Hadfield; 51 Miss J. Cree; 55, 74, The late W. J. Solloway; 60 Miss A. Wilkinson; 61, 66, 112, 128, 129, 143, 152 M. Marriott; 71 T. K. Harding; 75, 85 Mrs E. Simpson; 79, 102 J. Bone; 83 Mrs J. Romsey; 94, 101, 103, 105 The Manx Museum, Douglas; 95, 96 The Brooklands Society; 98 H. P. Hughes; 99, 100, F. W. Viles; 110 Vauxhall Motors Ltd.; 111 F. Williams; 130 J. L. Cam; 132 Pettipher & Son Ltd.; 133, 136 B. S. Ranford Ltd.; 137 *The Humber Register*; 147 H. Butcher; 156–8 R. Smith.

Introduction

Queen Victoria's long reign opened at a time when land transport was dominated by the horse and ended with the supremacy of the iron horse for, by the opening of the twentieth century, railways had established a countrywide network of an efficiency that was an example to the world. But the very efficiency of the railways served only to relegate the roads to a state of shameful neglect. The dominance of the horse entailed a whole social system devoted to the continuation of that dominance and to the preservation of the system itself which supported it and which represented a sizeable section of society that resented any threat to its own interests.

It was the bicycle that first posed that threat. Although the hobbyhorse, the first primitive bicycle of the closing years of the eighteenth century, was only a fad it did point distantly to future developments, developments which in 1869 took practical shape. It was in that year that The Coventry Machinists Co. produced 500 'boneshakers' of the Michaux pattern. These were the early hobbyhorses with the addition of cranks and pedals and with that challenge the threat to the horse took real shape, for within a decade British roads were to see the graceful high-wheeled 'ordinary' bicycles (later known by the nickname of 'penny-farthing') proliferate, and with them a wide variety of tricycles as well.

More importantly but less tangibly attitudes were changing too. The spread of railways changed the world by offering cheaper goods and wider horizons, but the railway passenger was tied to set routes and times. By contrast, the bicycle allowed complete freedom of choice as to distance and destination and a much wider radius of action than that of the horse. Seen against the background of Victorian society with its many restrictions, such freedom of movement made a considerable appeal. The importance of the bicycle in promoting a climate of opinion in which individual freedom of movement came to be thought of as desirable cannot be overestimated, for it was this, probably even more than the technical links between the cycle and the motor car, that paved the way for the motor age by the end of Victoria's reign.

By 1891 National Census Returns showed that Coventry alone could claim 4,039 persons directly employed as Bicycle and Tricycle Makers and Dealers, to which figure must be added a further 1,987 similarly employed in Birmingham and 643 in Wolverhampton, the West Midlands being the acknowledged centre of the industry. The re-invention in 1888 of the pneumatic tyre and its rapid adoption brought cycling to the forefront as a pastime. As a sport, cycling had a spectator appeal and a following akin to that of present-day football, and the extraordinary acceptance of cycling by society in 1896–7 gave it a respectability that many had been keen to deny it. Membership of the Cyclists Touring Club (C.T.C.) had more than doubled from 16,343 in 1895 to 34,655 in 1896. The ladies flocked to cycling and the freedom it gave them did more for the cause of Women's Lib than anything other than the political enfranchisement that they sought so ardently in the years up to the Great War and were not in fact to achieve until its aftermath.

The Victorians took their pleasures seriously with the result that determination, collective action and political lobbying by cycling interests performed a valuable social service by removing many legal anomalies and by setting up a properly organized consensus of information on cycling matters. It is to the Victorian cyclists that we owe the beginnings of a number of amenities that we take for granted nowadays: accurate and informative guides to localities; information as to the state of the roads, mileages, landmarks and beauty spots; a nationwide classification of hotels, boarding houses, taverns and refreshment rooms undertaken by the Cyclists Touring Club; and the erection of signs warning of road hazards. On this sound and comprehensive basis the tourists of the new motor age were to build.

Largely because of unrealistic and antiquated legislation concerning road transport, Britain lagged ten years behind her Continental rivals in the development of the motor car. But, as on the Continent, so in Britain too it was largely those long steeped in the world of cycling, as manufacturers, agents or riders, whose visions of future road transport centred on the motor car. Individuals too, particularly if they had money and influence, turned eagerly to the motor car and some, like the Hon. C. S. Rolls, racing cyclist as a Cambridge undergraduate and a motorist well before the turn of the century, were soon to turn their enthusiasm to powered flight in aeroplanes.

Naturally such far-reaching changes and social attitudes did not come about without resistance. Many saw the spread of cycling as a threat to much that they held dear and early motorists were to suffer an even greater unpopularity, even from some sections of cycling opinion. H. G. Wells wrote of his enjoyment of cycling, 'when there were no automobiles and the cyclist had a lordliness, a sense of masterful adventure, that has gone from him altogether now'. Many other critics were considerably more vituperative!

The 1000-Miles Trial of 1900 was the first large-scale motor event to take in virtually the length and breadth of the British Isles and it attracted huge crowds, thereby bringing the motor car before a larger public than ever before. Queen Victoria would have nothing to do with the motor car, but Edward VII, whose pattern of life showed in so many ways a desire to break away from the tight reins of matriarchy, accepted it eagerly, giving motoring a considerable social cachet allied to his own personal popularity. In Edward's short reign the technical progress of motoring was rapid and such progress naturally brought with it a much wider acceptance and use of the motor car. Motoring was no longer the preserve of the eccentric or the mechanical fanatic, and certainly of the rich, as had been the case at the beginning of his reign, and by 1906 there were some 45,000 cars in use in Britain; nearly 200,000 people had visited the Motor Show at Olympia that year, and the general election produced a record high poll in almost all parts of the country and was the first in which the motor car was almost universally used as an aid to candidates and electors.

By 1907 the number of cars had increased to 60,000 and the Edwardian heyday of motoring elegance was about to dawn. At no time since have contemporary fashion and contemporary motor cars been so ideally matched. Motoring costs were falling but for those who found the price too high (and who did not mind a degree of exposure to the elements that few car owners would tolerate even then) there was the motor cycle. The development of the motor cycle was immensely aided by the inauguration, in 1907, of the Tourist Trophy races in the Isle of Man, which were soon to establish an international reputation as a yardstick of performance and skill. The same year saw the opening of Brooklands Race Track, which did so much to redress the lack of racing facilities in this country by comparison with the Continent.

In present-day motoring parlance Edwardian motoring extends to 1918, and those few intervening years between King George V's accession and the Armistice of 1918 were of tremendous significance. Henry Ford's vision of 'motoring for the masses' began to be the dream of many in this country too but it was not to be realized, in this country at least, for another two decades and then only after the technical impetus of a world war in which the internal combustion engine was to take a leading and vital part for the first time. War brought a change in social attitudes even more cataclysmic, against which, in retrospect, the 1910–14 period is often seen as a dream-like Indian summer before the passing of an era.

Technically the cleavage between pre- and post-war motoring was less clearly defined than the change in the social environment. By 1914 the average motor car had a water-cooled monobloc side-valve engine, shaft and bevel or worm-drive, a three- or four-speed gearbox, and detachable wheels (with pneumatic tyres, of course). Electric lighting was reasonably commonplace except on the cheapest cars, and electric starting was available but far from widespread. Although open-body styles predominated, a good variety of body types was available at a wide range of prices and weather protection and comfort were entirely adequate. Advances such as overhead valves, single or double overhead camshafts born of the best pre-1914 racing practice, paid dividends in the aircraft engines of the war period and the forcing house of war brought about a tremendous improvement in metallurgical knowledge. Power-to-weight ratios improved significantly and aircraft engines had seen the introduction of aluminium pistons.

Such wartime advances were pointers to what lay ahead, but technical advances could seldom be instantly applied to the post-war generation of motor cars, so the immediately post-1918 cars were, by and large, the pre-war ones with updated details (and considerably updated prices!). Those years of Indian summer were the world from which the fighting men had gone, and for those who survived they were their precious link with sanity in a world gone mad. To many, that Indian summer included motoring in some form and motoring was a high priority in their post-war visions. The demands of war had greatly increased technical competence and awareness, so it is not surprising that the 1914–18 years were the gestation period during which the pattern of post-war motoring was developing, awaiting only the right conditions in which to be born as the lusty infant of the 1920s. The seeds of both technical development and the social climate that placed motoring high in the priorities had been laid in Edwardian motoring days and the post-war years were to show how generically strong those seeds were.

The photographs portray the many facets of this revolution in road transport and the social changes that accompanied it. One may recall—and wonder at—the unhurried calm of dusty village streets before the motor age when it was still safe to stop and gossip in the roadway without fear of death or injury; one may readily see 'that sense of masterful adventure' that Wells referred to reflected in the expressions of many a Victorian cyclist, sometimes transmuted to a grim determination to win on the race track. There are the ladies, some primly respectable and demure in their ankle-length skirts and decorative hats, standing proudly beside brand-new machines; others expressing the boldness of 'the new woman' in daring rational dress; there are the children (to whom cycling made an early appeal); and some of the more unlikely flights of imagination beloved of optimistic inventors.

Portrayed too are the many aspects of motoring from the early primitives, for which every journey was a compound of hope and doubt, to the powerful and elegant status symbols of latter-day Edwardian high life. The motor car itself is pictured in many guises—in the pristine splendour of its first creation and in the rusty shame of the scrapyard; as an adjunct to Royal occasions and as the humble accessory to a country picnic; in the hands of the famous and accompanied by drivers and passengers whose anonymity serves only to emphasize the transient nature of the human scene; in peace and in war.

In brief, the motor car had become intricately woven into our pattern of life. It had its detractors always, as it still has, and if visionaries of the motoring pioneers could have foreseen the problems the motor poses today the detractors would perhaps have been more! But the photographs are not presented to rewrite history, only to portray it.

Solid Struggle

The early years of cycling were a struggle, a struggle against legal anomalies, entrenched attitudes and social bias. Some 70 years were to go by between the earliest hobbyhorse machines of the 'Célerifère' pattern (1791) and the Michaux boneshaker with its cranks and pedals. From then on improving techniques gradually gave lighter machines and the constant desire for speed aided and abetted the quest for lightness. Thus evolved the high-wheeled 'ordinary' (penny-farthing), a machine for the young, the athletic, and the male. For the less athletic, for the older man or for the less venturesome—and for the ladies—there were tricycles, single, tandem or sociable (side-by-side), of dozens of different patterns and bewildering variety.

Bicycle and tricycle clubs multiplied and by the 1880s many cyclists were covering considerable distances, and journeys of 70–100 miles in the day were not uncommon. Many undertook tours of much greater length. Club riders, formally organized and strictly controlled by captain and sub-captain, enjoyed long trips into the country with halts at suitable hostelries, to return in the evening by the fitful light of oil or candle lamps aided perhaps by a full moon or else, lightless, risked the arm of the law. Already the speed of the bicycle was deceptive; a good ordinary skilfully ridden could easily outpace the horse over a longer range, and on its solid rubber tyres it was silent, a factor unnerving to pedestrians and other traffic.

By 1885 a number of attempts had been made to produce a machine that would not suffer from the drawbacks of the ordinary. None of these dwarf 'safety' machines had really caught on, but from then on the small-wheeled, rear-driven bicycle was to become increasingly significant. On 31 August 1888 Herbert E. Laurie became the first man to cover more than 21 miles in the hour on a bicycle. He used a rear-driven dwarf safety, a type which had hitherto not been regarded as any challenge to the established high-wheeler of the speedmen.

For road use, remembering the appalling condition of most roads at the time, the small-wheeled safety with its thin-section solid rubber tyres was vibrationary and uncomfortable, even though its design offered a freedom from 'headers' and a greater stability than the ordinary. The many types of spring-frame machines of this period were attempts to insulate the rider from vibration and road shocks, and Lindley & Biggs' Whippet was perhaps the most successful. But waiting in the wings, so to speak, to render all such devices obsolete and to seal the doom of the ordinary was the appearance of the pneumatic tyre. With its adoption the whole pastime of cycling took on a new dimension.

3 *Below, left* Members of the Facile Bicycle Club are seen here with John Beale (centre, wearing gloves), the patentee of the Facile bicycles. Although Beale took out his patents as early as 1869 the machines did not come into common use for some nine years. Notable in this picture are the scaled-down versions suitable for children

4 *Below* Between 28 July and 13 September 1889 Mr P. Hardwick, accompanied by his two young daughters Agnes and Edith, used the tricycle seen here for an extensive tour of much of Britain. Many adventures and misadventures befell them and one can only marvel at their hardihood

5 *Below* A braced cross-frame safety bicycle of *c.* 1889. Note the solid tyres, radial spokes, footrests on the front forks to aid 'coasting', which in pre-freewheel days had to be done with the feet clear of the flying pedals. Holding the machine is Mr A. D. Chambers, of Kidderminster, whose dog Poodie frequently accompanied him in this manner

6 Cycling clubs did much to encourage the pastime and, by their collective action, to improve facilities for touring and sport. The Royal Worcester Porcelain Works Cycling Club is shown here at its inaugural meeting in 1887. This was before the era of the pneumatic tyre and all these machines wear solids. There are tricycles in great variety, ordinaries, but apparently only one safety, on the extreme right

7 *Above* A charmingly-posed group of Victorian worthies photographed *c.* 1891. The gentleman of the party seems determined that his tricycle should be included and its front tyre shows signs of hard use. It is doubtful if any of the ladies other, perhaps, than the one in the straw boater, were practising cyclists

9 A group taken outside a large country house, 1892. What the benign old ladies think of the young man's spring-frame safety bicycle is not recorded, but he is obviously proud of it. The coming of the pneumatic tyre dramatically reduced experiments with spring-frame designs

8 Children with their tricycles at Temple Sowerby in 1892. The coming of the dwarf safety bicycle and the pneumatic tyre rendered earlier designs obsolete very rapidly. Many outmoded machines were handed down to the children

Floating on Air

Ridiculed at first (so often the fate of prescient novelties), the pneumatic tyre came at a most opportune time in the history of cycling. Despite its high cost in early years and the punctures inevitable on roads often little better than farm tracks, its advantages were great enough to ensure its rapid adoption. It added wings to one's wheels and within a few years the old solid, and the short-lived cushion, tyres were obsolete. Pneumatic tyres gave a tremendous boost to the safety bicycle which, by the early 1890s, had settled to a design that was to see almost no significant change until modern times.

With this new airy freedom of the bicycle the ladies began to play an increasingly important role. Their wider participation in the pastime was bitterly resisted by many (chiefly non-cyclists) and argument raged in drawing rooms and Press alike as to the propriety of ladies cycling. Lady cyclists often had to suffer abuse and even threats and physical violence. Those ladies who saw the unsuitability of contemporary fashion—with its voluminous skirts and tight waists—for serious cycling, and were brave enough to take to the 'abandoned' rational dress were almost universally criticized and, indeed, even ostracized.

Then, in the mid-1890s, cycling suddenly became respectable and for a few brief years, the 'in thing' when Society took to it and every lady of title and social standing was eager to be seen with her newest machine. Cycle manufacturers mushroomed; the larger, well-established makers were already turning

out tens of thousands of machines each year; the massive interest in the pastime was reflected in popular song, in the theatre and in periodicals and popular novels. Like all booms, this one had to decline, but by the end of it the nineteenth century was running out. New ideas, new freedoms were in the air; people were looking ahead to the twentieth century. Almost as quickly as it had taken to the bicycle society was agog for the newest toy—the autocar, which promised a new and greater excitement.

That the changes the new and exciting autocar was to bring would be so dramatic and far reaching was probably never envisaged by the majority of those pioneers of motoring who took to it. Cycling took a step down the social scale and was never again to enjoy the pre-eminence of those few years of the late 1890s. For its real devotees there were many more years of pleasure in store, and today we look again at cycling when we see the cost in lives and money, the traffic and parking problems, the noise and pollution and the threat to energy resources that the car inflicts on modern society.

But now, as the first autocars terrify the horses as they chug hopefully along the Road of Progress to the twentieth century, all that is in the future.

10 The dreaded puncture! Despite the common occurrence of this mishap in the early days of pneumatics their advantages so clearly outweighed such comparatively minor setbacks that solid tyres were quick to die

11 *Above* So widespread was cycling as a pastime by the late 1890s that even the most rural areas could usually boast an agent or, at least, a repairer. Mr. R. Cooke's Herefordshire premises boast a C.T.C. Repairer's plaque and enamel signs proclaiming 'Raglan and Enfield Cycles'. His own signboard terms him a cycle maker but most probably he assembled machines from the wide range of proprietary parts by then available

13 'The Anchor' at Ripley in the 1890s. Much favoured meeting place for cyclists, it attracted gatherings of many hundreds on occasions. In this picture one may note a 'lady-front' tandem and a triplet, in addition to numerous single safeties

12 *Left* It is difficult today to believe how quiet and unhurried most roads were in the pre-motor era. These cyclists are seen outside no. 2, High Street, Ingatestone, Essex, which presents a truly rural background. Such quietude is ably and amusingly mourned in Guy Boas' poem 'To a Bicycle Bell'

14 *Above* Victorian alfresco. This vivid portrait of a group of Victorian cyclists of about 1893 (the period of the safety bicycles seen leaning against the wall in the background) suggests a Sunday or Bank Holiday—and time to spare

15 In an attempt to stave off the 'dwarf' safety's popularity (a popularity so greatly enhanced by the pneumatic tyre) some late ordinaries were themselves fitted with pneumatics. This interesting machine is fitted with a front tyre of 46 in. × $1\frac{5}{8}$ in. and, surprisingly, has rim brakes and not the usual spoon brake acting on the tyre

16 Dress for lady cyclists was a burning topic in the 1890s! Full ankle-length skirts were customary and approved, but were not the most sensible or practical garments for serious riders. The latter, if brave enough, dared to wear 'rational dress': garments giving freedom of leg movement. The bulk of Victorian public opinion was outraged and many rational-clad riders suffered abuse and even physical violence. Rationals as portrayed here look purposeful, if not elegant

17 No rationals here! A lady cyclist of the late 1890s, a smart turnout. Apart from details of lamp and brakes, this lady's machine set a style that was to last almost up to the present and is still in widespread use

18 *Below* Transvestite? Mr Walter Santler pokes a little fun at the fashionable lady cyclists of the time at a Malvern Cycle Carnival, *c.* 1900. As an experienced cyclist himself he is perhaps also mocking the ladies' fondness for dressing up at carnivals and similar light-hearted events. Few ladies, however, would willingly have ridden a machine with as high a gear as this one—just look at that chain wheel!

19 A future Prime Minister is host to a local cycling club. Stanley Baldwin (seventh from the left, in straw hat) pictured with the cyclists and some of their machines, *c.* 1894

20 *Above* The Hon. C. S. Rolls, aged 16, with his bicycle in 1893. The lure of speed was to take Rolls through the realms of cycle racing (at Cambridge) to the motor car, in which he competed frequently in many of the great early classic events, and to the aeroplane, in which he was destined to lose his life. That his name should be linked to that of Royce and one of the world's greatest motor cars was really only incidental to his constant pursuit of speed

21 *Left* When the cycling pastime became the rage of Society in the late 1890s, manufacturers vied with each other to gain the patronage of the greatest number of crowned and princely heads and titled names. Here Edward, Prince of Wales, rides his cycle as a youth in 1911, by which time titled patronage figured mostly in the quality car makers' brochures

22 Sir Edward Elgar in many ways typified the Victorian, and more particularly perhaps the Edwardian, period. A man of many hobbies, he was an enthusiastic cyclist for many years, riding for miles around the Malverns and the neighbouring countryside, from which he confessed to have derived much inspiration for his music. Here he stands beside his brand-new Sunbeam in 1903. Note that the Sunbeam, which Elgar named 'Mr Phoebus', has three brakes, for Elgar was a tall and heavy man and Malvern a very hilly district

23 *Above* These three riders of the early 1890s might have been the models for Jerome K. Jerome's *Three Men on the Bummel*. Although better remembered for his *Three Men in a Boat*, Jerome was a keen cyclist and in December 1893 took the Chair at the annual dinner of the renowned North Road Cycling Club, whose members included some of the most famous in the history of cycling. The two flanking machines are on solids, that in the centre on pneumatics

24 These two windows featuring a special display of 'The New Departure Coaster Hub' form only a small part of the frontage of a large establishment in a superior part of town, *c*. 1906. A cycle agent such as this carried extensive stocks of parts and machines and could deal with virtually any eventuality

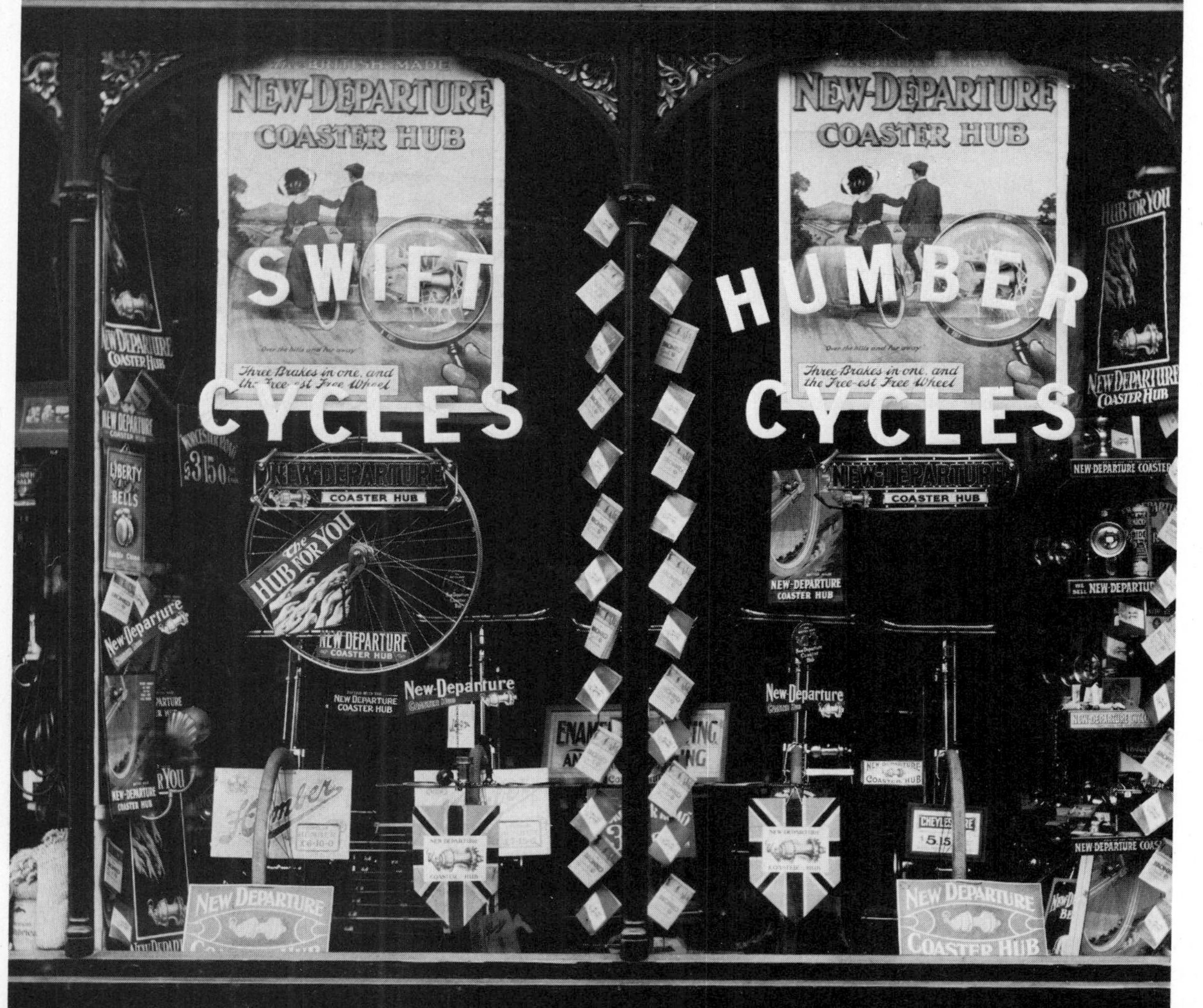

ER. REPAIRER & ENAMELLER. 69
NEW-DEPARTURE
COASTER HUB
Three Brakes in one, and the Free-est Free Wheel
SWIFT
CYCLES
HUMBER
CYCLES
THE HUB FOR YOU
NEW DEPARTURE COASTER HUB
LIBERTY BELLS
New-Departure
NEW DEPARTURE
COASTER HUB

25 *Above* When cycle racing was at the height of its popularity many towns built cycle race tracks, though by no means all were as good as the Carmarthen one seen here at an event in 1906

26 Few achieved the distinction of representing their Country in international events but to those who did the Public afforded eager acclaim. Here, from left to right, are C. B. Kingsbury, Leon Meredith, Ben Jones and Ernie Payne who formed the winning British Pursuit Team at the 1908 Olympic Games in London

27 Military cyclists of the 1890s. Members of the 4th Hants Cyclists (Volunteers) pose with their machines. Men such as these were to prove the worth of the bicycle in military use in the Boer War

28 *Above* A ceremony in High Town, Hereford, to mark the end of the Siege of Mafeking. Clearly visible among the militia are the military cyclists, their machines each carrying a rifle. Most counties boasted a Cycle Section attached to a local Volunteer Regiment

29 Always popular with the ladies, decorated cycle parades enjoyed a long vogue. Unusually, we see here an all-male cast, soldiers of the Worcestershire Regiment at Norton Barracks, who have displayed considerable ingenuity of costume for their Bicycle Costume Race of 1897

30 *Above* S. F. Edge, one of the greatest racing cyclists, seen here (centre) in a strange device known as the Hydrocycle, of 1890. In front of him is F. Cooper and astern is R. W. Smith, all well known in cycling circles. Edge became one of the foremost pioneer racing motorists and was a man of considerable energies and influence. The boat (?) was built by Hammertons of Long Ditton

31 *Left* A bicycle of *c.* 1892 fitted with handgear. Intended as an additional power factor for hill climbing or when strong headwinds were encountered, the device was described by a contemporary cycling journal as 'a rather cumbersome invention'

32 The cycle industry, like others, produced some strange freaks from time to time, sometimes in pursuit of novel ideas, sometimes in attempting novel methods of tackling known problems. This one was purely for advertisement and was sure to catch the eye! Portrayed here is a Humber Eiffel tandem of *c.* 1897. The cycle agent's premises form the background and it is the agent himself who is bravely seated up aloft

33 A main street in a cathedral city before the motor age. Summer sun, a pony and trap in from the countryside, horse manure littering the street, one or two cyclists visible (cyclists are well catered for—note the sign 'Beds for Cyclists') and not a motor in sight. No wonder there was opposition to the new-fangled motor!

Against the Odds

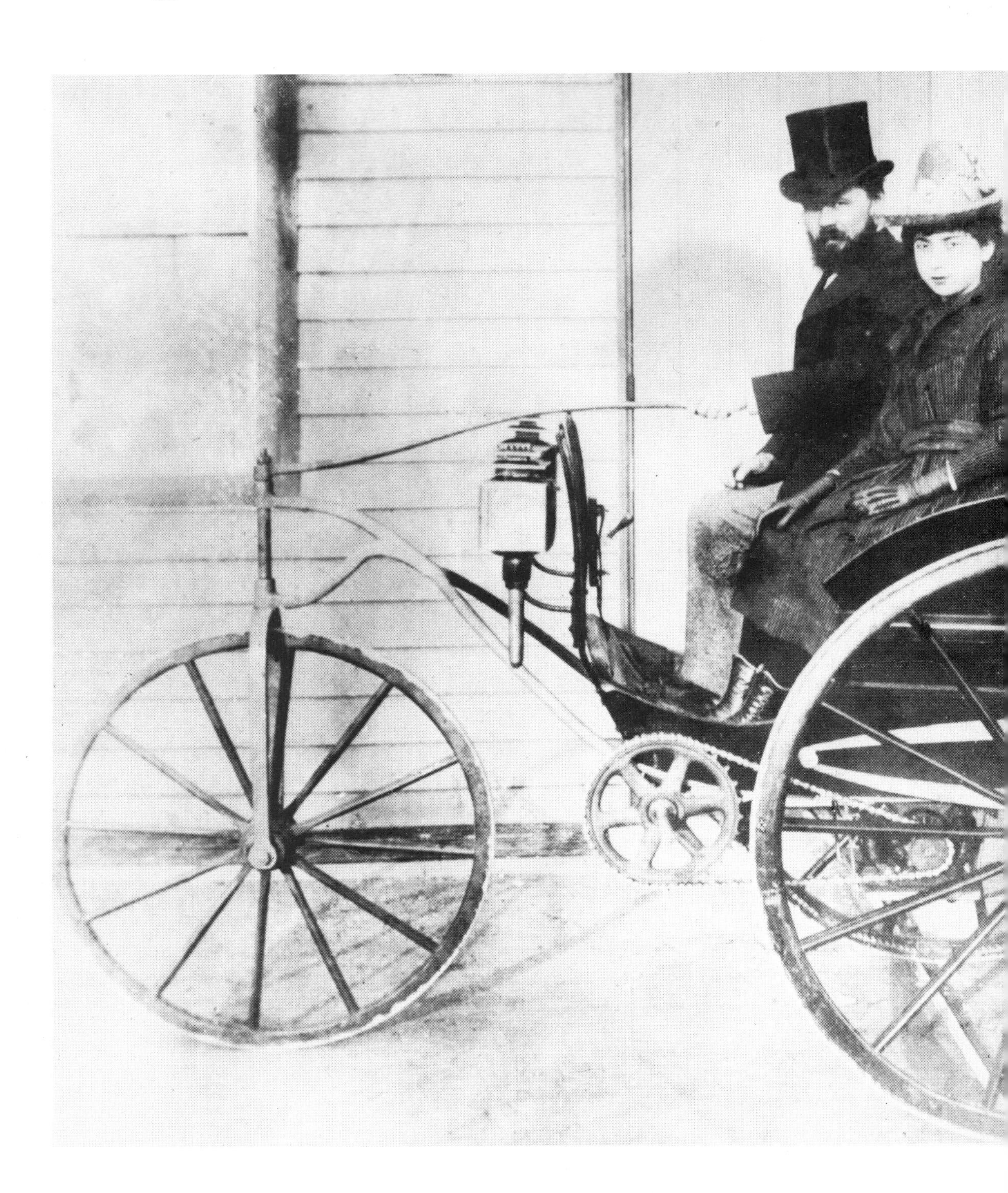

Pioneer motorists of the last decade of the nineteenth century had to contend with almost as much opposition as had the early cyclists, and this despite the significant change in outlook that the spread of cycling had accomplished. They had also to contend with machinery that was often temperamental and of which they themselves understood but little. Even worse, they had to contend with legislation that was outdated, complex and often maladroitly applied. So, assuming the motorist of the time was wealthy enough to purchase an autocar (of foreign manufacture, incidentally, there being virtually none of British make available) he would have to risk the arm of the law, the scorn of his horse-and-carriage friends, the chance of a breakdown in some out-of-the-way spot with no help forthcoming, and the hostility and ridicule of the general populace (albeit this was tempered by a little awe and wonderment at times).

Prior to the Locomotives on Highways Act of 1896 which legalized motoring in Britain, there were few indeed in this country who had attempted to use a motor vehicle and fewer still who saw any future in trying to make such a thing. The restrictions imposed prior to this Act had already allowed France and Germany a head start in the manufacture and use of self-propelled vehicles. But a few men of vision and some, less scrupulous, whose vision extended only to their own enrichment by the floating of dubious companies and by sharp financial dealing, were actively promoting the cause of the motor car in this country prior to 1896.

At a time when any motor car was experimental, reliability was not a strong point and two particularly troublesome features were ignition systems and tyres. Despite the obvious success of pneumatic tyres for cycles many doubted that they could withstand the greater weight and higher speeds of the motor car. By the turn of the century, however, their use was increasing though by no means universal, but they were a very expensive item. They wore quickly, and until detachable rims—and later, detachable wheels —became normal, tyre troubles were many and the

34 Magnus Volk, better known for his novel electric tramway at Brighton, is seen here at the tiller of his electric dog cart of 1887. Neither its steering geometry nor its final drive arrangements inspire confidence, but it was at least a self-propelled vehicle

curing of them an unpleasant and exhausting chore.

In these early years of struggle the majority of motor cars in this country were imports from France or Germany or less frequently from other European countries. The French firm of De Dion Bouton and the Belgian firm of Minerva were early in the field as exporters of proprietary engines of various capacities, ranging from those suitable for a lightweight motor cycle to bigger units capable of propelling a small to medium-sized car. Many budding British manufacturers without facilities or unwilling to make their own engines turned eagerly to this source of supply. Remembering that these European makers had the advantage of years more motor experience than their British rivals, their products were in general entirely satisfactory by the standards of their time, and the lessons learned from this foreign expertise were to be incorporated in the great technical advances that were to come about in the following decade.

On the social front opinion was sharply divided: a minority welcomed the motor car either because it seemed to hold prospects of almost revolutionary progress or more often because it was an exciting novelty; the majority, because it was unfamiliar, noisy, smelly, potentially dangerous, terrified the horses, or for a dozen other reasons of greater or lesser validity, were determined to oppose it. However, because at that time the motor car was essentially for the rich, and because wealth spells influence, the effect of the welcoming minority was soon to be felt by the hostile majority. As always, ignorance and unfamiliarity with the true 'nature of the beast' brought prejudice; the years immediately ahead were to see a long struggle as increasing technical progress brought more and more motor cars into use in Britain while motors and motorists gradually overcame the prejudices of the anti-motoring lobby. Both the motor car itself and attitudes to it were to mature.

35 *Facing page* A $1\frac{1}{2}$ hp Benz of 1896—the first car in Middlesbrough. Despite the 'horseless carriage' epithet it shows many features that derive from cycle practice rather than from equestrian tradition—the tubular frame, radial-spoked non-detachable wire wheels, pneumatic tyres and even the primitive brake acting directly on the tyre

36 *Right* Its cycle ancestry very apparent, this 1900 Progress Quadricycle with $2\frac{3}{4}$ hp De Dion engine was the proud possession of a Cornish owner. It was later registered AF 77 under the Motor Car Act of 1903

37 Amidst much publicity the Hon. Evelyn Ellis took a party in his Daimler to the summit of the Malvern Hills on 12 October 1897. Ellis is seen holding his granddaughter who lived in Malvern until very recently. Note the solid tyres and primitive spoon brakes of this early autocar

38 *Above* An assembly of motorists and their cars and motor tricycles gathered outside the Town Hall, Wells, Somerset on 15 October 1901. The occasion was a quarterly meeting of the Somerset County Council when a motion before the meeting urged a petition recommending the registration of motor vehicles. The motion was carried!

39 Charmingly evocative of the early years, the dashing young driver seems a little apprehensive despite the adulation of the ladies! The Gladiator car, though not new, carries no registration plate, so the picture must be prior to 1904, registration plates being compulsory wear after 1 January of that year. The picture suggests that it was posed for the occasion and in all probability the car was motored no further than back to the motor house afterwards

40 This early single-cylinder Humberette shows clearly the cycle influence of its parent firm, who had an outstanding reputation as cycle makers long before they embarked on motor production. This model and others generally similar put Humber 'on the map' as motor manufacturers

41 *Below* Posed outside the works in Malvern Link where it was built, this 6hp Santler was one of a very small number of cars built by this pioneer between, it is alleged, 1887 and the early 1920s. The designer and builder, T. C. Santler, is at the wheel, and almost the entire workforce of this small concern is represented in this picture, *c.* 1902

42 Hazy winter sunshine illumines this posed group while a very young lady is permitted to take the wheel of this early Benz

43 The same young lady, a few years older now, proudly grasps the wheel of her very own pedal car, *c.* 1910

44 In the early days many were far from convinced that the petrol engine was best for powered locomotion. Steam cars, however, needed a knowledgeable and understanding driver to get the best out of them. This White steam car is about to depart from Moraston House, Ross-on-Wye, in the summer of 1903

45 *Below* Closed bodywork was uncommon on early cars because it was weighty (particularly if as ornate as this example) and thus handicapped an already often limited performance. This elegant Panhard et Levassor's covered top is detachable, however, above the waistline, making the car readily adaptable to winter or summer use. The chauffeur stayed in the open whatever the season

46 *Right* Typical of the transitional stage when many an established cycle-dealer was taking on motor work, this garage clearly reveals its origins. James Fryer, 'the boss', sits at the tiller of the 5hp Oldsmobile on the right, and the other car is a 12hp Gladiator. Most of the pedal-cycles are Humbers, as is the right-hand motor-cycle. The year is 1903

47 This 16hp 2-cylinder Albion of *c*. 1904 was a product of a Scottish firm that soon abandoned the private car for the commercial field, in which it had a long and successful career. This model's specification and equipment were even then (1904) surprisingly outdated and the car lacks any form of weather protection

FRYER
MOTORS
CYCLES
FRYER

Acceptance & Growth

By 1905 the motor cars of the pioneering period had developed sufficiently for a clear pattern to emerge from the welter of experiments. By and large the system developed by Panhard—a front-mounted engine, the gearbox abaft it, and transmission, usually by side chains but with the 'live' axle (that is, the shaft to a bevel or worm differential) a growing contender, to the driven rear wheels. With detail modification this was to be the norm for several decades.

Engines had become increasingly powerful, goaded by the god of speed. The usual method of obtaining increased power was by increasing the bore and stroke, or the number of the cylinders. Crankshaft speeds remained low and the notion of obtaining greater efficiency from engines of smaller capacity by increasing crankshaft speeds had to await a better understanding of metallurgy and more advanced techniques of construction and balance, together with better design of the combustion spaces and valve layout. As in the immediate past, it was the quest for speed in racing cars that initiated technical advances and the lessons learned from racing were gradually incorporated in general design.

The higher speeds attainable by the average road car of the period made improved weather protection imperative, to say nothing of the need to protect the driver and passengers from the menace of the dust on the roads of the time. Suspension too became a more important consideration as road speeds increased. Cars of the Edwardian period were no longer the short-wheelbase, shallow-doored, rear-entrance tonneaux of before, with their high centre of gravity, near-vertical steering columns, and lack of hood and windscreen. By 1914 the average open touring car had entirely adequate weather protection, the tall and majestic Roi des Belges body had given way to the lower, uniform line of the 'torpedo' and driver and passengers now sat in, rather than on, the car.

Improved performance now made practical a wide variety of body styles, open, closed or convertible. The majority of closed bodies were both heavy and four square, but it must be remembered that closed bodies were mainly used for formal occasions when etiquette demanded formal dress. The top hats of the gentlemen and the lofty creations of the ladies dictated an equivalently high roof line for limousines and landaulettes. However, by 1914 a number of coachbuilders were successfully turning out closed bodies of grace and symmetry without undue sacrifice of headroom.

By 1914 the motor car was altogether a much more refined machine—mechanically as well as in appearance and appointments—than its predecessors of ten years earlier. To take a rather extreme example, one has only to compare the immortal Silver Ghost Rolls-Royce of 1907 with a luxury car of but two or three years earlier to gauge how real the process of improved technique and refinement had become.

This technical progress and the rapidly increasing use of motor cars that resulted from it at first brought increasing anti-motoring pressure to bear, and to offset this the motoring organisations, whose membership was growing apace, were becoming more collectively and politically active, just as the cycling organizations had become when faced with opposition a generation or so previously. Motoring costs began to drop and the emergence in about 1911 of a new breed of cheap lightweight cyclecars, largely derived from motor cycle practice, emphasized forcibly that for all but the largest luxury cars running costs were now less than the costs of maintaining a single horse and trap or carriage.

The old domination of the horse and the attitudes it engendered were slowly being eroded. It was to take the cataclysm of war to set the seal on that process of erosion and war was far from the thoughts of most motorists on pleasure bent in the opening years of King George V's reign. The golden years blossomed on . . . endlessly, it seemed.

48 This early Mercedes was owned by a wealthy Cornish family who, it seems, were enthusiastic enough to take it on an extensive motor tour embracing Scotland, where it is here portrayed on the road between Dalmally and Crianlarich

49 An early Peugeot of 12hp seen about 1903 near St. Austell, Cornwall. Note the stowage of the spare tyre

50 *Above right* Brand new and spotless, this Aberdeen-registered Peugeot with swing-seat tonneau body has the shaft drive newly introduced for their 1904 models. Its driver is clad to combat the elements, the car itself lacking any such protection

51 Many early motor cars were not fast but they did stir up a great deal of dust in their wake when the weather was dry. As speeds increased some form of weather protection was essential and cars began to be fitted with windscreens and hoods. This car, believed to be a Decauville of about 1903, boasts neither. The occupants wear plenty of clothing and the ladies' caps look precarious but would have ample hat pins. In an emergency these could be used to clear choked petrol pipes or carburettors!

RS·5
WORKS
GARAGE

THE SPA HOTEL RESTAURANT

52 *Left* The height of one-upmanship in registration numbers! This little Wolseley bears the first registration issued in Co. Leitrim. Car and occupants pose confidently while the hotel domestics and the sidecar driver (placating his horse) watch the camera

54 New Radnor is a quiet little village on the main road from the Midlands to Aberystwyth and the Welsh coast. When this photograph was taken, *c.* 1904, it could have seen but few motors, so the Wolseley (left) and the Panhard have attracted numerous onlookers

53 *Left* The first electric brougham in Cambridge. Electric power found some favour from the earliest days for town cars on account of its silence, reliability and lack of smell and pollution. Limited range was, as it still is, a drawback and electricity soon ceased to be a practical rival to the petrol engine. This example is an Opperman of late 1903

55 *Above left* This 10-vertical-twin Royal Enfield of 1904 is typical of the light cars of the time. The makers had an enviable reputation as cycle makers before entering the motor field by way of tricycles and quadricycles fitted with proprietary engines. As car makers their career was short lived, but they continued to enhance their reputation in cycles and motor cycles. Note the motoring rug that warmly protects the lady driver's legs

56 *Above* An early Panhard et Levassor with rear-entrance tonneau body poses against the photographer's favourite backdrop of Hereford Cathedral

57 The forecar was a motor-cycle-derived machine that had a short-lived popularity from about 1901 to 1907. Protection from the elements was minimal, though a waterproof apron over the fore carriage, as here, was not uncommon. Since it was often a lady who occupied the front seat it was unfortunate that she should be so vulnerably placed in the event of an accident

58 The little Wolseley seen here is halted in rural Herefordshire. Motorists and cottagers alike face the camera with stern concentration

59 *Below* The passengers in this early Swift look as rugged as the background of the East Pool Mine, Camborne, Cornwall

60 The family poses in the little two-cylinder Wolseley, a successful and popular model that had a long run. The tyres and tubes carried in front of the radiator tubes emphasize the bogey of the puncture and the chore of tyre changing with non-detachable wheels. Tyres, even for a light car, were a major expense in the early days of motoring

62 *Left* This 1907 15hp Humber is pictured at a period when it was customary to have to pay extra for such items as hood, screen, lamps and horn when purchasing a new car. These items would have added at least £50 to the basic cost of this model at £340

61 *Left* Despite the ample buttoned-leather upholstery this Vulcan boasts little weather protection, so the driver is wrapped warmly in rug and topcoat and wears gloves

63 Scottish product in Cornwall. This Argyll landaulette, owned by a Mr Daubauz, a wealthy mine owner from Truro, is a splendid example of the make. Argyll was Scotland's most successful make, at one time being the fifth largest motor manufacturer in Britain, but they overreached themselves and rapidly declined after 1918

64 *Above* This Sizaire–Naudin, one of the earliest makes to adopt independent front-wheel suspension, is seen in Kent, far from Scotland where it was registered

66 With the god of fire himself as a mascot, this Vulcan car of 1911 has a touring body of a shape that remained recognizably similar for many years. For a long time to come open cars outnumbered closed cars but, except for the most sporting types, a windscreen and hood were considered essential

65 *Above* The Edwardian period has been described by some as being one of ostentatious vulgarity. In its motor cars, however, it often achieved a dignity that has never been surpassed. This Daimler, a make given Royal patronage, posed in front of the quiet orderliness of a country house, has no hint of vulgarity about it. The flags would seem to hint at a special occasion, but there is no clue as to what it might be, unless it were King George V's coronation

67 *Left* Farewell to a guest, perhaps? The luggage in the tonneau suggests that the lady passenger is about to be accompanied to the station. The lady at the wheel is probably not a driver but is merely posing in the driving seat for the picture, for she seems to be eyeing the chauffeur a little apprehensively

68 *Below* A British disciple of the engine-before-radiator school that for so long typified Renault, this handsome Siddeley–Deasy was photographed at St. Ives

69 Opposite poles of greatness unite in a common cause. On the left Henry Ford's immortal Model-T and on the right a Rolls-Royce Silver Ghost, both on active service in the Great War. In many ways a prophetic picture foreshadowing the blurring of social distinctions that the motor car did so much to bring about

70 Swords into ploughshares! This ex-R.F.C. Crossley, of which large numbers were in use during the war, has reverted to civilian guise as a 25/30 landaulette. Like many post-armistice cars it was purely Edwardian in concept

Motor Cycling

71 *Above* Early clip-on; a proud young owner displays his new Singer motor wheel in 1905. Introduced some years earlier by Messrs Perks & Birch and taken up by Singer, this self-contained motor wheel unit could be fitted to any bicycle or tricycle frame. Tricycles wore their motor wheel in front

72 This 1904 Quadrant motor cycle tows a passenger trailer, a precarious device in which the long-suffering passenger was exposed to all the dust and fumes. Even worse, it was not unknown for the trailer to come adrift and the motor cycle rider to be unaware of it. Trailers of this type soon gave way to the sidecar

The earliest motor cycles were largely a development of the pedal cycle in that the basic pedal cycle frame was the structure upon which an engine, with its accessories and controls, was hung. The high frames of such machines made such motor cycles prone to sideslip and difficult to control, particularly as little thought was given to weight distribution by the somewhat haphazard way in which engine and accessories were attached. For a time, about the turn of the century, motor tricycles and quadricycles found more favour on account of their greater stability. Among the more successful early machines was the Perks & Birch 'motor wheel' which was a self-contained unit that could be fitted to any cycle or tricycle frame and which had the advantage of keeping the centre of gravity low.

Most early motor cycle engines were crude and unreliable and developed little power; transmission systems often lacked any clutch and were single geared; ignition and carburation were unreliable and braking ineffective. However, the introduction of belt drive, which eliminated the coarseness of direct-gear drive and gave a much smoother transmission, albeit with the attendant risk of belt slip and some loss of power, and the increasing availability of more powerful and reliable engines led to much-needed improvements in frame design. These developments opened up new horizons for the motor bicycle and the motor tricycles and quadricycles began to lose favour.

Phelon & Moore introduced chain drive in 1901 and the Belgian firm of F.N. were early in the field with shaft and bevel drive, but the majority of machines made use of belt drive, either direct or from a primary chain. Most early machines had auxiliary pedal drive, both for what was euphemistically termed 'light pedal assistance' when ascending hills and for starting purposes. By far the majority of machines were lubricated on the constant-loss principle, oil having to be fed at regular intervals to the crankcase by means of a handpump with sight feed from an oil tank on the machine, usually a compartment of the petrol tank.

From about 1905 technical development was rapid and the speed potential of the motor cycle was recognized by many. Improved techniques and greater reliability began to influence others than the diehard devotee, and many who could not afford a motor car but desired the mobility of motor transport found the economy and handiness of the motor cycle attractive. Nevertheless, exposure to the elements, while of little moment to the enthusiast, was something of a bugbear to the rider who wished to take a passenger. The early forms of passenger trailer were far from ideal and were soon succeeded by the more satisfactory sidecar, in which the passenger was at least out of the direct wake of the machine's exhaust fumes and the road dirt and dust flung up by its wheels.

Passenger work highlighted the snags of the single-gear machine, particularly in hilly districts, and the first decade of the twentieth century saw a proliferation of variable-gear devices. Early forms were more robust forms of the hub gears found on pedal cycles, though a number of makers introduced other forms of variable gear. One of the most successful of these was the Rudge-Multi with its 'infinitely variable' form of belt drive. In the years immediately prior to the Great War a few firms were offering two- or three-speed countershaft gearboxes, and some indeed offered all-chain drive. In a few cases, notably the Sunbeam, the transmission was entirely enclosed and thus protected from dirt and wear.

In this period manufacturers mushroomed in Britain, on the Continent and in the USA. In 1910 there were 86,000 motor cyclists in Britain and by 1913 this number had doubled. The British industry began to make up for its late start. The inauguration of the Tourist Trophy Races in 1907 did much to foster technical progress and to focus attention on British machines. By 1914 British machines were being as widely exported as had been their foreign rivals in earlier years. The seed that was to grow into the world supremacy of British motor cycles in the 1920s was already being purposefully cultivated.

73 *Left* Although this V-twin Rex was first registered in Glamorgan the photograph was taken in Herefordshire. The unusual form of front fork springing and that of the lamp bracket are worthy of note

74 *Below* B.S.A.—initials long famous not only for armaments but for cycles and their components. The prototype B.S.A. motor cycle is here ridden by Richard Nicholls, works manager at the Redditch premises formerly used by part of Albert Eadie's Royal Enfield 'empire'. The year is 1910, and the early form of trade plate may be noted

75 Chiefly because the motor cyclist was so exposed to the elements, few ladies took up the pastime in the early days. Some did, however, perhaps seeing it as an extension of the degree of female emancipation that had brought thousands of women to cycling a decade or so earlier. Here, two sisters of the famous Stevens family of Wolverhampton flank a mere male with their machines, c. 1911

76 *Left* This 1910 $3\frac{1}{2}$ hp Rex, seen here almost immediately after it was first registered on 7 February of that year, presents a much tidier and more orthodox appearance than its stablemate of only a year or two earlier (illustration 73)

77 *Right* A Phelon & Moore (P & M) combination of *c.* 1912. P & M were early pioneers of chain drive and of an inclined engine built into the frame. Astride this machine is 'Ixion' of *The Motor-Cycle*, one of the best-respected and, through his writings, best-known of all motor cycle enthusiasts

78 Many early motor cycles that sold widely in Britain were foreign imports, some of the most popular being the Belgian Minerva and F.N., the French Peugeot and the Motosacoche from Switzerland. The N.S.U. was a German make that achieved much popularity and which was available with a very successful two-speed epicyclic pulley gear, as on this machine

79 *Below* Most sporting motor cyclists have dreamed up their ideal machine but comparatively few have translated their dream into physical reality. Seen here is a 5/6 hp twin-cylinder Wright–Blumfield, a sporting machine made in small numbers *c.* 1912 by a Kidderminster rider, A. C. Wright

CB-632

CB-138
CB-632

Rudge
CB-138
CB-632

80, 81, 82 *Left* A pleasing sequence illustrating the brotherhood of the road, always strong among the motor-cycling fraternity. The two Rudge riders are strangers to the district; their machines are well-laden, they pore over the map. Local knowledge comes to their aid and their informant, himself a motor cyclist, poses with them amid grateful smiles

83 *Below* A group of works testers from the A.J.S. and Sunbeam works gather informally in the countryside near Wolverhampton. George Dance (left) for Sunbeam and Frank Giles (second left) for A.J.S., were later to achieve considerable distinction as competition riders

84 Quite a number of amateur riders assembled their machines from proprietary parts, but few could have been as unorthodox as this example, a De Dion-engined machine built in 1909 and portrayed in that year

85 Even established makers sometimes experimented with some odd ideas. This big-twin A.J.S. of 1915, with Joe Stevens at the sidecar controls, was one of a number of somewhat similar machines produced by A.J.S. and others in an attempt to improve the scant degree of weather protection afforded to the motor cyclist

86 *Left* An early Morgan cyclecar. This Malvern make hit upon a design that was simple, cheap and relatively robust which, coupled with an ardently-pursued and successfully-advertised competition programme in which they indulged, led the Morgan to become an outstanding machine destined to outlive all its cyclecar contemporaries

87 *Below* Most cyclecars derived much from motor-cycle practice. They enjoyed an initial boom from about 1910 and another, due to the inflated economy of the post-armistice years, in the early 1920s. This very rare machine, a Santler Rushabout, was made in Malvern and bore a more than superficial resemblance to the much better known Morgan. The Santler did not share the Morgans' successes

88 A Grand Prix Morgan of 1914. A fast, exciting machine, it was only by keeping it moving fast enough that the driver had any protection from the elements! Its sporting clerical owner probably, if he was wise, removed the parsonical shovel hat before moving off

May the best man win

The motor car had barely assumed physical existence in penny numbers before someone hit on the idea of promoting a competition in which motor cars competed against each other. That someone was M. Pierre Giffard, a French newspaper proprietor who initiated the world's first motor competition. This took place in the form of a 'race' from Paris to Rouen in July 1894.

In this, as in motoring in general, France was a leading pioneer. Not for another two years was motoring even legal in this country, and even after The Locomotives on Highways Act of 1896 legalized it, the idea of unrestricted speed on public roads was anathema to the British Constitution! In the next seven years Europe saw, for example, the Paris–Marseilles of 1896, the first Gordon-Bennett Race from Versailles to Lyon of 1900, the Paris–Bordeaux and the Paris–Berlin of 1901 and the Paris–Vienna (of which the Gordon-Bennett Race formed part and which provided, as a result of S. F. Edge's technical win, a portent for Britain) of 1902. These great races formed a publicity platform for European manufacturers and drivers and were invaluable experience in a period of rapid technical improvements. During all this time no comparable event could, or did, take place in Britain.

The 1000-Miles Trial of 1900 was, by contrast with the city-to-city races in Europe, a tame affair and in any case in no sense a race, but it did much to bring a number of widely-varying motor cars to the notice of the Public. However, S. F. Edge's victory for Napier in the 1902 Gordon-Bennett placed Britain in the position of being honour bound to act as host country for the next year's Gordon-Bennett event. To bring this about, considerable bending of existing legislation had to be achieved, even to hold the event in Ireland. No town-to-town race this, (at least Britain was spared the increasing carnage such races caused, and the attendant recriminations) but it was run over seven laps of a course centred on Athy, giving a total distance of 327½ miles. The whole event was the first true race of an international calibre ever held on British soil, but Napiers, the sole British entrants, fared badly and victory went to Jenatzy in a German Mercedes.

Apart from speed trials, hill climbs and, of course, reliability trials, Britain's legal anomalies forbade the 'excesses' indulged in on the Continent, though even there the carnage caused in the Paris–Madrid Race of 1903 forced second thoughts. This country had to await the farsightedness and public spirit of H. F. Locke King and the coming of Brooklands Race Track in 1907 before unrestricted speed could be unleashed and even then Brooklands was not to assume international importance for some years.

On the Isle of Man, however, though still British soil, the authorities were more enlightened, and for specific periods public roads could be closed to normal traffic and races held thereon. In 1904 the first British Eliminating Trials for the Gordon-Bennett Races were held there. Thereafter the island assumed considerably greater importance as the 'home' of the motor cycle Tourist Trophy Races from 1907. Car events of this type were held there in 1905 to 1908 and again in 1914, with a final fling in 1922, but the motor cycle series has run unbroken, except for wars and their immediate aftermath, ever since.

Sport and competition in any form have always exercised a particular fascination and appeal to the British people. The circumstances outlined above may have denied Britain many of the plums in the period under review, but the eagerness of British motorists and motor cyclists to indulge in motor competition could not have been greater. The outbreak of war in 1914 virtually killed off such activities, as it killed, alas, so many of those addicted to them. But by 1914 thousands of keen motorists were competing in serious but friendly rivalry, and sometimes on a shoestring budget, merely for the love of the thing.

Every weekend, particularly in summer, would see a wide variety of events up and down the country. These events ranged from important Brooklands races, or sprints and hill climbs at which perhaps expensively backed works entrants would compete, to those attended, maybe, by only one or two minor clubs entirely made up of amateurs; from carefully-prepared record attempts to sprints on sandy beaches at those seaside resorts lucky enough to have a wide expanse of sand exposed at low tide.

Because of the excitement of contest and the spectator appeal, photographs of motor sporting events are perhaps more abundant than those of other specifically motoring activities. The best of them capture, as words cannot, the challenge, the excitement and, in early days, the novelty of such events; they capture too something of the risks and misfortunes attendant on them. The question has often been posed as to why people put themselves and sometimes others at risk in pursuit of some challenge. Perhaps among the many reasons the sporting motorist might give the underlying one is because the challenge exists.

89 *Left* All the dust and fury of the early road races. Percy Owen and his mechanic Graham defeat the wind-cheating outline of their 40hp Winton Bullet, which, like the other American entries in the 1903 Gordon-Bennett Race in Ireland, failed to finish

90 The 1000-Miles Trial of 1900 covered much of the length and breadth of Britain and brought the new motors to the notice of many of the Public for the first time. The late St. John Nixon, himself a participant, wrote of dense crowds that congregated three and four deep in all the towns through which they passed. Competitors here approach Maidenhead

91 *Right* Early streamlining! Gabriel's Mors approaches The Moat, Ardscull, Athy, during the 1903 Gordon-Bennett Race. 'To facilitate its report of the race,' as *The Autocar* put it, that journal arranged for 'a captive balloon at a convenient place upon the course'

92 *Right* The 1903 Gordon-Bennett Race was held in Ireland as a result of S. F. Edge's win for Britain in the event of the previous year, thus giving Britain the right to act as host for the 1903 event. It was staged in Ireland to overcome the intractable laws of this country governing racing on the public roads. It was Camille Jenatzy, seen here with his Mercedes, who won the 1903 event for Germany

93 Lady drivers were rare indeed in competition in the early days, particularly in Britain. Here Miss Dorothy Levitt, a chic and successful competitor whose mechanical knowledge and sound commonsense impressed as much as her charm and good looks, acknowledges the approval of the crowd as she sets off from Hereford High Street during the Small Car Trials of 1904. Her car is a De Dion Bouton

94 *Right* Eliminating Trials for the Gordon-Bennett Races of 1904 and 1905 were held in the Isle of Man, whose legislature was more liberally minded than our own. Seen here is the 100hp Siddeley out on the course some days prior to the 1905 event. It did not qualify for the Gordon-Bennett Race itself

95 *Left* The opening of Brooklands heralded a new era in British racing; portrayed here is Roy (later Sir Roy) Fedden in a Straker-Squire after finishing first in the All-Comers Handicap on 1 August 1908. Sir Roy was later to achieve fame in the field of aeronautics

96 *Left* The Napier came swiftly to the front in racing circles and did more, perhaps, than any other British make to keep British prestige high prior to 1914. In 1907 Brooklands Track was opened and a racing Napier in the hands of Frank Newton is seen here at Brooklands in that initial year

97 *Below* Saltburn Sands, Yorkshire, saw Frank Newton achieve 102mph in his 90hp Napier Meteor on 27 June 1908. Extensive sandy beaches were popular for speed events and record attempts but sand and salt spray were very injurious to machinery

98 *Right* Approaching the start of a speed hill climb at Coalport, Shropshire, in 1911. Jack Stevens of A.J.S. fame is on the extreme left and is wearing the same cap, jacket and waistcoat that he wore at the T.T. in that year. The machines had just been weighed in at the G.W.R. Coalport station before tackling the climb

99 Members of the Redditch & District M.C.C. halt at the Stanford Bridge Hotel in the Teme valley in the course of a road trial, *c.* 1913. In the foreground a large rider of a big Matchless combination studies the map and the inevitable small boys look on

100 The spectators are all eyes as they watch one of the competitors raise the dust as he takes a sharp bend on one of the roads climbing the Cotswold scarp during a speed trial, *c.* 1914

101 *Left* First held in 1907, the motor cycle Tourist Trophy Races in the Isle of Man rapidly came to be regarded as the most testing of any, both for machines and riders. Reputations were made or lost on those tortuous miles and successful entries gained considerable prestige. Here machines line up for the start of the 1913 event. The Revd E. P. Greenhill of The Auto-Cycle Union is seen on the left beside no. 25, a Douglas; nos 88 and 129 are Indians

102 *Above* The Isle of Man was the scene of Tourist Trophy Races for cars also, though these did not survive for anything like the length of time that the motor cycle events have. Here the Light Twenty Rolls-Royce entered for the 1906 event line up to make use of the rather primitive form of petrol pump. The leading car, no. 4, was the winner of the race, driven by the Hon. C. S. Rolls

103 An excellent close-up of the 16/20 Coventry Humber entered for the 1907 T.T. and driven by W. G. Tuck. Unfortunately the car burst a tyre and broke a wheel in the penultimate lap and did not complete the course

104 Nineteen-fourteen was a significant year, not only because of the lurking shadows of war but because it saw competing for the first time on British soil examples of the new school of racing design inspired by M. Henry for the 1913 Peugeots. Humber and Sunbeam entries for the 1914 T.T. closely followed the Henry school, but by contrast the Belgian firm of Minerva remained faithful to the double-sleeve valve. They did well in the race, gaining second, third and fifth places, but were unpopular with their rivals on account of the dense clouds of oil smoke they left in their wake. This is C. Riecken's car in front of the smokescreen

105 One can see rather more of the car in this shot; this is L. Molon's car, no. 2 of the Minerva team

106 *Above* Product of a firm long established in engineering before taking to motor manufacture, Crossleys were beautifully made, stolid, conservative cars. Apart from toying with front-wheel brakes almost earlier than anyone they were seldom venturesome. This splendid example built for the 1914 T.T. and driven in that race by Cecil Bianchi is here portrayed in their Manchester works

107 *Below* Economy, light weight and simplicity were said to be the strong points of cyclecars, though many were crude, unreliable and highly uncomfortable. This dramatic shot shows a sporting Buckingham cyclecar tackling a speed hill climb at Caerphilly, *c.* 1914, and epitomizes the cult

108 All the fun and fury of an Edwardian speed hill climb! This splendid Vauxhall storms up Shelsley Walsh on one of the occasions when that famous hill was dry enough to produce a dustcloud. Few pictures better convey the spirit of the time and the particular atmosphere of this Worcestershire hill

109 *Above* A light car, descendant of the *voiturette,* at the Caerphilly hill climb. Light cars scorned the crudities of the cyclecar and were large cars in miniature. Such sporting versions as this little Mathis were the forerunners of the small sports cars of the 1920s

110 A fine car by any standards, this Pomeroy-designed 'Prince Henry' Vauxhall was one of the first true British sports cars. J. A. Barber is seen here at the wheel during a hill climb run by the Herts Automobile Club at Aston Clinton, near Aylesbury

37
V-1500

Picnics & Pleasures

It is probable that the first motor picnic has not been recorded for posterity and it is certain that pleasure is a very personal idiom, for what is pleasure to one may be boredom to another or distasteful to yet another. Rather, then, one must consider this title as a generic term to express the conditions that apply when the motor is used for what insurance companies drily call 'social, domestic and pleasure' purposes; when, in fact, it is not being used primarily as a demonstration of the efficiency of a machine, nor in competition, nor yet as a means of getting from A to B in a certain time.

It is a title to express a certain harmony—a harmony that exists when the purpose is enjoyable and suits the mood of the moment and the motor car blends the two together and yet, at the same time, does not intrude its personality, or the lack of it, as a machine in its own right.

For such a state of harmony to exist—and surely if it does not the pleasure is spoilt—it follows that the motor car must have attained a certain degree of comfort and reliability. Here too one is on uncertain ground, for both comfort and reliability are relative to personal tastes. No doubt some pioneer motorists active in the stage of the motor car's development that I have earlier referred to as compounded of hope and doubt, did consider some, if not all, of their motoring as a pleasure; they may even have picnicked! Certain it is that the later Victorians and more particularly the Edwardians regarded the picnic as both pleasurable and socially acceptable. What more natural, therefore, that when the motor car gained some degree of social acceptance it should unassumingly take its place in such pleasurable activities?

The photographs in this chapter form an interesting paradox in that the motors portrayed, though often in the foreground, are really a background—an accepted adjunct to an event and not its primary purpose. From the viewpoint of the social historian this paradox is as significant as is the mechanical marvel and its potential for change to the transport historian. For in this context the tide has turned, not when the novelty—motor car or what you will—is treated as a novelty or a challenge or an instrument of change, but when it is accepted into the fabric of daily life.

Our pre-1914 motorists are doing just what the motorists of today are doing; going to the pub, going on an outing, stopping by the roadside for a picnic, visiting friends, going on holiday perhaps. They are a mirror of their time, but are probably unaware that their easy acceptance of the motor in such activities was to be a portent for the future.

111 A pleasing family motoring scene of the Edwardian period. The car is a Reo, an American importation made by Ransom E. Olds, formerly of Oldsmobile

112 *Below, left* The Wesleyan Mission sets out on a three-day autumn motor tour. If all the gay-bonneted ladies are going to travel they will need more than the three cars seen here, but it is more likely that they have come to give the travellers a good send-off and to have their photographs taken

113 *Below* A summer picnic in that fateful summer when the war clouds gathered, 1914. The car is a new Humber 10 hp and the location the Forest of Dean

114 Picnic *en masse*. A 1910 12hp Humber forms the backdrop for this summer picnic in that year. Running boards were always useful either, as here, as improvised benches or as convenient stands for the picnic gear. The motoring dog is not a modern phenomenon

115 Picnic *en famille*. The same family, but friends not invited on this occasion, and with a different car and dog. The car is a 1914 Humber 10 hp and the location is the Malvern Hills

116 Few present-day motorists would picnic under these conditions, for the trees are innocent of leaves and a chill wind ruffles the pennant on the Rudge-Multi's handlebars. Another Rudge combination and an air-cooled Humberette have joined the party

117 *Above* The guns of peace. A Napier shooting-brake is framed by members of a party shooting on Lord Montagu's Beaulieu estate, *c.* 1911. Lord Montagu, an influential pioneer motorist, is standing second gun to the right of the car

118 One hopes that the little Humberette's brakes were up to the task! The notice to cyclists warning of the steep hill is a reminder of the pioneer work of this kind undertaken by the cyclist organizations that was to be so beneficial a legacy to the motorists

119 *Above* Sunbeam and Renault shimmer in the sun of of an Edwardian summer beside Knaresborough's Mother Shipton Inn. The Sunbeam's chauffeur may have been an abstainer but more likely he slipped into the public bar for a quick one after the photographer had finished

120 *Left* Inns have traditionally catered for travellers and the coming of the motor car added considerably to their trade. The Fish Inn, Broadway, was and still is a well-known landmark at the summit of the Cotswold scarp. The hill presented a real challenge to early cars but their cooling systems at least could be replenished after hours!

123 *Right* Sunshine, summer clothes and the seaside—to many an idyllic combination. This picture of *c.* 1913 reminds us that the motor car opened up such delights to many, while it aptly suggests the somewhat fragile peace of the immediately pre-war years

121 *Above* The details of this picture give a good idea of current fashions in weather protection pre-1914. The Rudge-Multi combination sports a wicker sidecar with claustrophobic hood (unusual at this period); its passenger, the lady in the foreground, wears a full-length waterproof coat and helmet and goggles, and beside the machine her husband wears clothing typical of the time for the all-weather motor cyclist

122 The same two machines and personalities in another setting, this time one of the picturesque villages of the Vale of Evesham. The Humberette cyclecar wears an early form of trade plate and the motoring dog is visible in both pictures

Make & Mend

This title disclaims any connection other than the most tenuous with the similar nautical expression; it signifies only that for the spread of motoring to occur there had to be those who made and those who mended, and no survey of the motoring scene can safely gloss over this fact. Both the makers and the menders existed in guises covering every shade of the spectrum, from the short-lived opportunist to the controlled expansion of a well-found concern; from the grandiose (many of whom overreached themselves) to the humble, even verging on the squalid.

Though British motor manufacture began well in arrears of that on the Continent, here—as there—it developed for the most part from successful cycle manufacture. There were, of course, notable and successful exceptions, but the origins of these latter usually lay in other forms of engineering—Lanchester, Napier and Rolls-Royce, for example. Despite a late start technical development in the British industry was on the whole of a high standard. In the USA, by contrast, technical development lagged behind European standards but, by the years immediately prior to the Great War, American production figures were surprisingly high. The concept of mass production fascinated the American motor industry long before it was taken up in Britain or in Europe, thanks most of all, perhaps, to the vision and dynamic energy of Henry Ford (I), whose Model-T had achieved production figures, and a time/cost ratio per unit, undreamed of outside America.

And what of the menders? Theirs was in many ways an unenviable task, but a vital one. It fell to dealers and agents and even to the self-styled Motor Expert (alias blacksmith, perhaps) of provincial towns and villages to act as the buffer between a distant manufacturer and a dissatisfied and sometimes irate customer. By his immediate personal contacts the small-time agent or repairer, if skilful both as mechanic and amateur psychologist, could do an immense amount to foster good relations and thus the spread of motoring. Conversely, such a man, if incompetent, could greatly harm the pastime. This would, of course, also be his own undoing.

The wealthy and those who owned 'snob' motor cars, whether of British or foreign manufacture, often scorned to make use of the local agents or repairers but had their drivers regularly return the motor to the manufacturer's works for major overhauls. In those more leisured times when labour was cheap and plentiful this was not unpractical, but one hesitates to contemplate the degree of upheaval such a thing would cause today!

The photographs reveal the diversity of the premises used, particularly by the menders. In the period under review few motor dealers' premises were purpose built, but rather were they a hotch potch of adaptations of buildings originally erected for a variety of other purposes. Frequently access to the workshops was through narrow arched entrances and passageways through which the lofty limousines and landaulettes of the time could scarcely squeeze. Only in the most opulent establishments was there adequate showroom space; the norm was an overcrowded shop front with room for perhaps one or two cars on display and a plethora of accessories and advertisements. There may well have been some facilities for lock-up accommodation, usually at the rear of the premises. Despite such apparently unsuitable quarters, it is surprising that quite humble establishments often turned out first-class mechanical work and were fully prepared to tackle lengthy and complex overhauls.

In short, the makers and menders were the means by which a social and transport revolution was achieved. They were also the means by which the dreams of the inventor were given a practical form. One could say that they were the means of changing a way of life.

124 *Above, right* Learning the hard way! The Hon. C. S. Rolls, spanner in hand, stands purposefully beside his first car, a $3\frac{3}{4}$ hp Peugeot of 1896. Pioneer motorists had to be self reliant as there were few who could advise them. One hopes it all went together again!

125 *Below, right* An interesting view of the interior of C. S. Rolls & Co.'s workshops at Lillie Hall, West Brompton. Established in 1902 when the Hon. C. S. Rolls went into partnership with Claude Johnson, these extensive workshops dealt with a flourishing motor business as well as working on Rolls' Mors and other racing cars long before the historic link with the name of Royce

126 *Below* This 1905 photograph is full of interesting detail. The motor cycle on the left (FK 68) is a Rex, and the one behind it is probably one made on the premises and known as the Worcester Road. Note also the crates for 'petrol'—a term coined by Carless, Capel & Leonard, whose exclusive right to the word forced Pratts to term their product Motor Spirit. The cramped premises are typical of many at the time

127 *Right* Typical of the transition from cycle dealer to motor repairer, this Hampshire garage interior of *c.* 1904 shows work in progress on a Panhard, while on the right a cycle frame is being brazed and 'the lad' trues a cycle wheel. Advertisements for Townend and Imperial cycles and for B.S.A. fittings adorn the wall

128 *Right* A delightful plethora of enamel advertising signs adorns the walls and the pile of wooden crates obstructing the pavement contain petrol cans, in those days (1904) delivered by rail. The car is another example of the popular and successful De Dion Bouton

B.S.A

CARBURINE
MOTOR SPIRIT
A.W. MARRIOTT
CYCLE ENGINEER
MOTOR EXPERT
LUCAS'S
A 6733

129 A line of cars with a wagonette on the right outside a garage premises, *c.* 1905. 'Royal Albert' is a survival from the cycle days of this firm, one of whose ranges of machines was thus named. The firm is still extant but no longer in these premises

131 *Right* A splendid study in facial expressions! Portrayed is the interior of a Hereford garage about 1909. The 'Gov'nor' in the tweed suit is Mr Butcher, seated centre. The number of men present and presumably on the strength of this medium-sized provincial garage gives some indication of the cheapness of labour in the Edwardian era

130 *Left* This unusual machine, registered FK 84 on 10 June 1905, was built by the man at the wheel, J. J. Cam, a partner in the Cam Engineering Works of Worcester. For many years a keen cyclist, Mr Cam was one of many with an engineering training and background who in the early years of the motor car decided to 'do it yourself'. His cars never went into serious production, however

132 *Right* The cycles in the left background were the firm's own make, The Compton. The forecar with its wicker seat and the motor cycle are of interest, and it will be seen that the firm also traded in sewing machines

AGENT. FRYER'S GARAGE. HEREFOR

DUNLOP
TYRES
PETTIPHER'S
MOTOR
CYCLE
WORKS

134, 135 A keen young rider snapped in his father's garage premises, *c.* 1911. The machines are a $3\frac{1}{2}$ hp Humber with Roc two-speed hub gear (illustration 135) and a $3\frac{3}{4}$ hp Indian of that year. This model Indian swept the board in the Senior T.T. in that year

133 *Left* The little Royal Enfield lightweight has its virtues proclaimed on the window placard. The legends 'Machines for Hire' and 'Private Track for Teaching' are a legacy from the cycling boom of the 1890s when any self-respecting agent offered such facilities. Phonographs were among the sidelines carried by this firm

136 *Right* Interior of a Malvern garage, *c.* 1914. The initials 'M.E.' appearing after the proprietor's name stood for Motor Engineer or Motor Expert, qualifications widely used but in some cases of dubious value. As this firm survived in the same ownership until very recently one assumes that the appellation was well deserved!

137 *Below* An interesting scene inside the Humber Works at Coventry late in 1913 or early 1914. Despite the serious expressions some had no doubt been chaffing the photographer as he climbed aloft to take the picture

138 *Above* Exorcism? A Rolls-Royce Silver Ghost is laid bare in an army workshop during the war. The look of puzzlement on the sergeant's face and the untidy array of parts and tools makes one wonder if the makers' own exacting standards are being adhered to

139 Incendiarism? Could this be the unfortunate owner glumly reviewing the sorry remains of his burnt-out motor in the battered and charred debris of the motor house? This misfortune occurred near Henley-on-Thames in August 1909, and in all probability this car was never repaired

Occasions

'A special time or season'; 'a chance of bringing about something desired'; 'a special ceremony'—thus the dictionary defines, among other definitions, the word 'occasion'. If there is indeed a common denominator in the definitions I have quoted, perhaps it is a desire to see and to be seen, no matter whether the occasion is of special significance to few or to many; to those who take part it is a time for display and for spectacle.

For great State occasions, in this country at least, the horse still reigns supreme. For the State processions, a coronation, a Royal wedding, a State funeral, we cling still to an ancient pageantry. By contrast that dreadful phenomenon of our age, the motorcade, is a sorry substitute. A stream of identical luxury limousines, flanked by a phalanx of motor cycle outriders, tailed by supporters and hangers-on, rushes madly forward in a high-speed, security-conscious age and leaves in its wake a rather nasty taste.

Somewhere in between these two extremes lies our title as concerned with the motor car. Our occasions still have their own dignity and their own sense of display. Perhaps it was the assassin's attack at Sarajevo in 1914 that cruelly opened the eyes to the risks of what in the ugly terminology of the second half of the twentieth century we call the motorcade. The majority of our occasions portrayed in this chapter occurred before that rude awakening, and indeed, that they should be the means of perpetrating violence, political or otherwise, would have been totally repugnant to those taking part.

As for the motor cars, they too had to express a sense of ceremony and display. Almost invariably it was the most opulent available that were chosen to take part and, of course, they were cleaned and polished to show off all their resplendent finery: the polished brass, nickel or even silver would catch and reflect every gleam of light; the paintwork shone with a deep, fruity glaze which the lining-out pointed and amplified; and the drivers' and attendants' uniforms were their best and neatest. Often the cars would themselves be decorated, perhaps with the colours and emblems of a political party if the occasion was one of politics, or with flowers and garlands for a wedding, (a happier inspiration than the white ribbons and bows which even in Edwardian times were coming into fashion). Tyre walls, even, might be whitened.

Speed was of no concern. Rather was it pleasant and desirable to travel slowly, so that those within the motor car or cars could be better seen by the spectators, so that the Royal personages could acknowledge their subjects' cheers, the bridal pair could wave to friends and relatives who could share the joy of the occasion, so that the parliamentary candidate could be seen to best advantage by those whose votes he hoped to win.

So—join in, and from the best vantage point that you can find enjoy our occasions—without defining them.

140 A beflagged car waits outside the main entrance of a hotel while the man of the moment and his supporters on the balcony above acknowledge the crowd

141 The motor car, as much as the house in the background, signifies a move up the social ladder as compared with illustration **142**. The car is a chain-driven Mercedes and will probably convey this pair of newly-weds for the whole of their touring honeymoon, even if their ultimate destination is the Continent

142 *Below, left* Country wedding. It is high summer in rural Herefordshire, the flags and posies are out in full force, as are the friends and relations. How much more pleasant to see this hired Edwardian landaulette itself decorated with garlands rather than the white ribbons customary today. After several more photographs have been painstakingly grouped the bridal pair will trundle to the station and their honeymoon will have begun

143 *Below* A rare make to be found as a hire car in a cathedral city, this 40/50 Gobron-Brillié was first registered on 11 November 1911 as CJ 997. This make, with an illustrious history in early racing, long supported the dubious claims of opposed-piston engines with all their resultant complexity. Portrayed here as slightly modified a few years later, the car is taking a bridal pair from the reception. Let us hope their ways were not to be as opposed as those of the Gobron's pistons!

144 The motor car in politics. Parliamentary candidates and their agents were quick to realize the advantages that a motor car could bring in electioneering, particularly in far-flung rural constituencies. Here the Hon. Tony Robarts of Lanhydrock is seen in a decorated Wolseley near Brunel's Saltash Bridge during an election campaign

145 Two Lanchester cars in the foreground of a political occasion when the man of the moment is Mr Chamberlain, in the leading car. Lanchesters were startingly original in conception and design but the stubbornly conventional attitude of the buying public and interference from his Board of Directors forced Frederick Lanchester to abandon both the 'bonnetless' look (the engine was almost wholly within the front compartment), and the side-arm, or tiller, steering seen here in favour of the accepted norm. So much for politics in the Board Room!

MR. JAMES
ROWLANDS'S
CENTRAL
COMMITTEE ROOM.
DARTFORD DIVISION
PARLIAMENTARY ELECTION, 1906
VOTE FOR
ROWLANDS.
IT'S TIME WE HAD A CHANGE!
CLOSED DOOR
JAMES
ROWLANDS
VOTE FOR HIM
MR. JAMES
ROWLANDS'S
CENTRAL
COMMITTEE ROOM.
VOTE FOR
ROWLANDS
THE TORIES

146 *Left* The general election of 1906 was the first time that motor cars had been extensively used in an election campaign. Mr James Rowlands, Liberal Candidate for the Dartford Division in Kent, is here about to tour his constituency. The car is a 1905 16/20hp Beaufort

147 *Left* Prince Henry of Prussia, younger brother of Kaiser Wilhelm II, was an ardent and influential motorist who gave his name to a series of long-distance 'tours' or trials held in Europe from 1908 to 1911. Only in the latter year did The Prince Henry Tour include a British route as well as a German one, and here the Prince himself, at the wheel of his Benz which he drove throughout the event, is welcomed in Hereford on 18 July 1911. The Prince Henry series of trials were the genesis of a number of famous sporting models of Continental and British make

148 *Above* The Prince and Princess of Wales in Cornwall on 18 July 1903. They visited the first Marconi wireless station at Poldhu on that day

149 Royal Daimler of 1905, a 35hp Hooper limousine, poses outside York Cottage with the Prince of Wales, later King George V

150 Daimlers are still the Royal cars and the setting is the same as in illustration **149**, but now, in 1911, it is the youthful Edward, Prince of Wales, who is seen at the wheel of the leading car. This picture makes an interesting contrast with illustration **22**, taken in the same year

The Chauffeur's Lot

Sir W. S. Gilbert wrote that 'a policeman's lot is not a happy one', but what of that of a chauffeur? Chauffeur—the very word is by derivation a misnomer, denoting by implication a fireman or stoker, rather than a driver. Yet perhaps this ambiguity of cross-channel translation and usage may alert one in some degree to the ill-defined position the chauffeur occupies in motoring society. Nowadays one thinks of a chauffeur-driven car either as being immensely long, immensely shiny, the prerogative of the immensely rich, or, alternatively, as the embodiment of the anonymous impersonality of a procession of sleek but identical fleets of hire cars that may be summoned at immense cost by those who, for one reason or another, do not see fit to use their own, or public, transport. But it was not always so.

Just as in horse-and-carriage days those who could afford a handsome turnout relied on the services of a coachman and groom (the former added status, the latter attended to the chores), so in the early days of motoring there were many wealthy enough to take to the new pastime who were nevertheless reluctant to acquire its skills and still more reluctant to take on its chores. Thus there grew up two fairly clearly-defined branches of professional drivers, or chauffeurs; the one, ex-coachmen or grooms, perhaps, whose masters had taken to the motor car and who expected them to adapt themselves to the driving and care of it; the other, made up of the younger and more adaptable men in most cases, those who had 'got in' to the motor business in some way and perhaps had a fair smattering of mechanical knowledge and who opted for the better wages, frequently with accommodation found, and the 'glamour' of private service. For those who found private service unattractive or were unsuited to it, there were, as motoring spread, many jobs in taxi work and provincial hire.

In retrospect it is easy to see the glamour side of the job; the opportunities for travel and the appeal of being seen, sometimes in High Society, at the wheel of a costly, powerful and immaculate motor car. It is easy to overlook, however, the foibles and idiosyncrasies of some employers; the often lengthy and sometimes unreasonable hours; the many more hours

151 This confident chauffeur standing beside an almost brand-new 15hp Coventry Humber of 1908 would certainly have started as a lad in the traditions of horse transport

spent in waiting, the car at the ready, while the master or mistress dallied over business or social life; and the chores. Few motor cars of the pre-1914 period showed any consideration for the convenience of their drivers. Quite apart from an almost universal lack of weather protection for the paid driver (no matter how luxurious the rear compartment) most cars, large ones in particular, required a formidable amount of daily and weekly care if they were to be kept in the tip-top condition the makers inevitably considered essential. As well as regular attention to engine, gear-box and back-axle lubrication, a large car might well have upwards of 50 greasers or lubricators on the chassis that required daily or weekly attention. Clutches had often to be 'dressed', brakes adjusted, bearings checked; at frequent intervals decarbonization was needed, valves had to be ground, and that common bugbear, the ignition system, carefully looked over.

A very wealthy employer, owning several large cars, for example, might well employ two or more chauffeurs and a full-time mechanic or mechanics as well, but the majority of chauffeurs were chauffeur–mechanics and were expected to cope with all but major mechanical overhauls in their stride, as well as having the car or cars impeccably turned out and punctually available when required. Until the advent of detachable rims and later, wheels, tyre troubles were frequent and coping with them a tough, dirty and exhausting business. By no means were all employers sympathetic when troubles of one kind or another beset them on their journeys even if the chauffeur was entirely innocent of any dereliction of duty.

There were, of course, unscrupulous chauffeurs who would take advantage of their employer's ignorance of the details of motoring and would obtain parts and services at cheap rates and charge the full amount to the employer and in various ways surreptitiously feather their own nests. But a good chauffeur, competent and trustworthy, could usually rely on a secure position in which he had the confidence of his master and the respect of his fellow servants. His trusted position often enabled him to indulge his own taste in motor cars to some degree by carefully influencing the choice of his employer when it came to buying a new car. Indeed, long and faithful service and an appreciative employer not infrequently led to a comfortable bequest should the chauffeur still be in service when the employer died.

Often it would fall to the chauffeur's lot to instruct 'the young master' in the art of driving, and though the young master might well be something of a nuisance in his constant badgering to be allowed to drive (when under the legal age, perhaps) many a young man has had lasting cause to be grateful for the impeccable grounding in driving and mechanics that was passed on to him by the family chauffeur, even if on occasions the local constable had to turn a knowingly blind eye to the activities of young so-and-so from the big house. Somehow one cannot imagine that impersonal uniformed driver of today being quite as ready to oblige—and with today's traffic conditions, perhaps that's just as well!

152 *Left* By the early years of this century the motley array of hansoms, growlers and hotel buses with their sometimes seedy-looking nags was being invaded by the motor cab. Some versions of these deliberately copied the outlines of their horse-drawn counterparts, but by 1910, about the time of this picture, most provincial cabs were standard landaulette bodies on normal chassis. Here a Belsize (left) and a Humber await their fares on a cab rank at a provincial station

153 *Above* A French make with a long competition history, this handsome Mors touring car awaits its lucky owners, who appear very pleased at the prospect. The somewhat unusual position of the speedometer is obviously intended to catch the chauffeur's eye

154 *Left* Daimlers typified the chauffeur-driven tradition for many years. This Cardiff-registered example proudly boasting an AA badge on its radiator cap and a Gabriel exhaust whistle above the nearside running board epitomizes the Edwardian period as ably as do its occupants

155 *Left* The luggage on the roof rack is carefully sheeted and roped, the two spare tyres covered and strapped, and this fine Napier landaulette seems all set for a lengthy journey. It is not too easy to decide whether the daughter of the house (one presumes) is eyeing the photographer or the white-coated chauffeur!

156 *Above* The chauffeur had his chores as well as the glamour of being seen at the wheel of fine cars. Here the second chauffeur, jacket and waistcoat removed, cleaning cloth in hand, stands beside one of his charges, a 1907 12hp Arrol-Johnston in the motor house

157 *Below* The big Edwardian Napiers exuded an air of almost conscious superiority. This particularly fine example had been supplied to its proud owner by Frank Newton, one of Napier's well-known racing men (see illustration 95). A white coat and cap cover were *de rigeur* as summer wear for the chauffeur, or on celebratory occasions such as weddings, even in private service

158 *Right* This 30hp Sheffield-Simplex seen here when almost brand new in April 1914 was a noble example of Edwardian engineering, beautifully built and notably quiet and refined to match its elegance. No wonder the chauffeur looks proud of his master's choice (or perhaps his own opinion was consulted?)

FK 277

159 Finale: snow casts a chilly blanket on the sorry remains in a mechanical graveyard. An era passes